THiS CoLoring BooK BeLONgS Too

——————————————

LIAMA FUN

FUN IN THE SUN

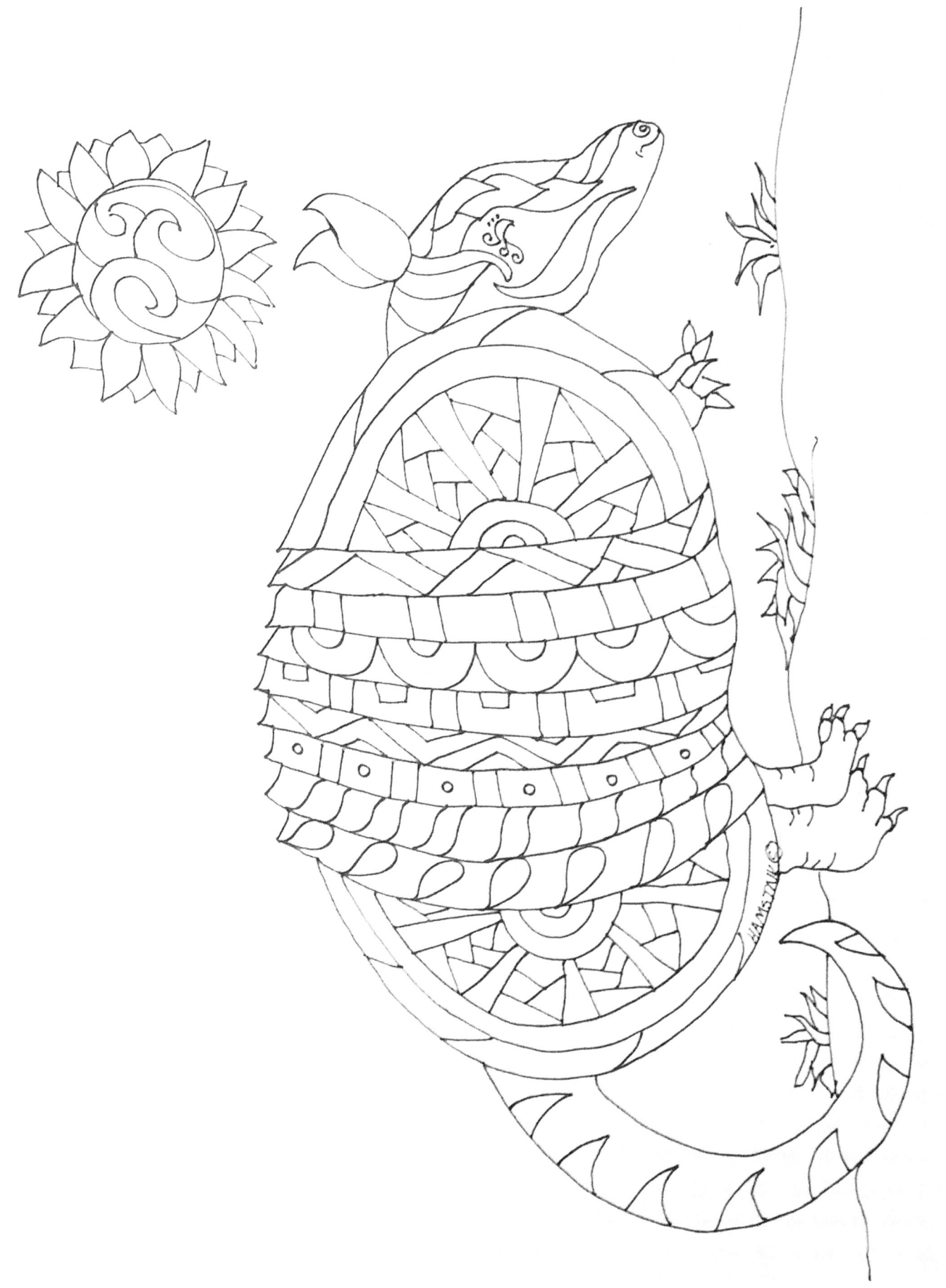

SMILE AND THE WORLD SMILES BACK

NATURE'S BUTTERFLY LOVE

THE CAT'S MEOW

HAPPY DAYS OF LOVE

RELAXING FUN

SUMMER BUTTERFLY

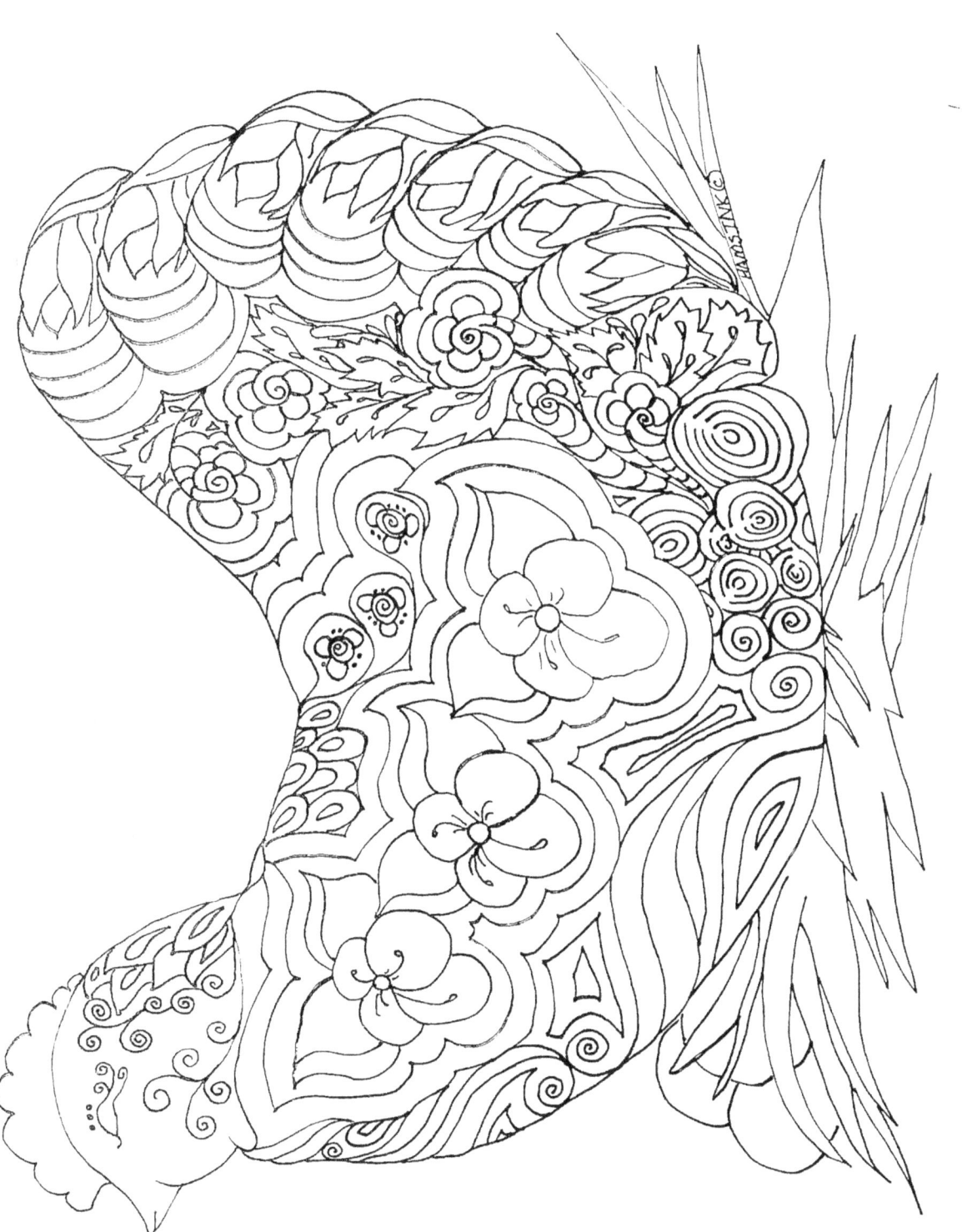

FARM FUN

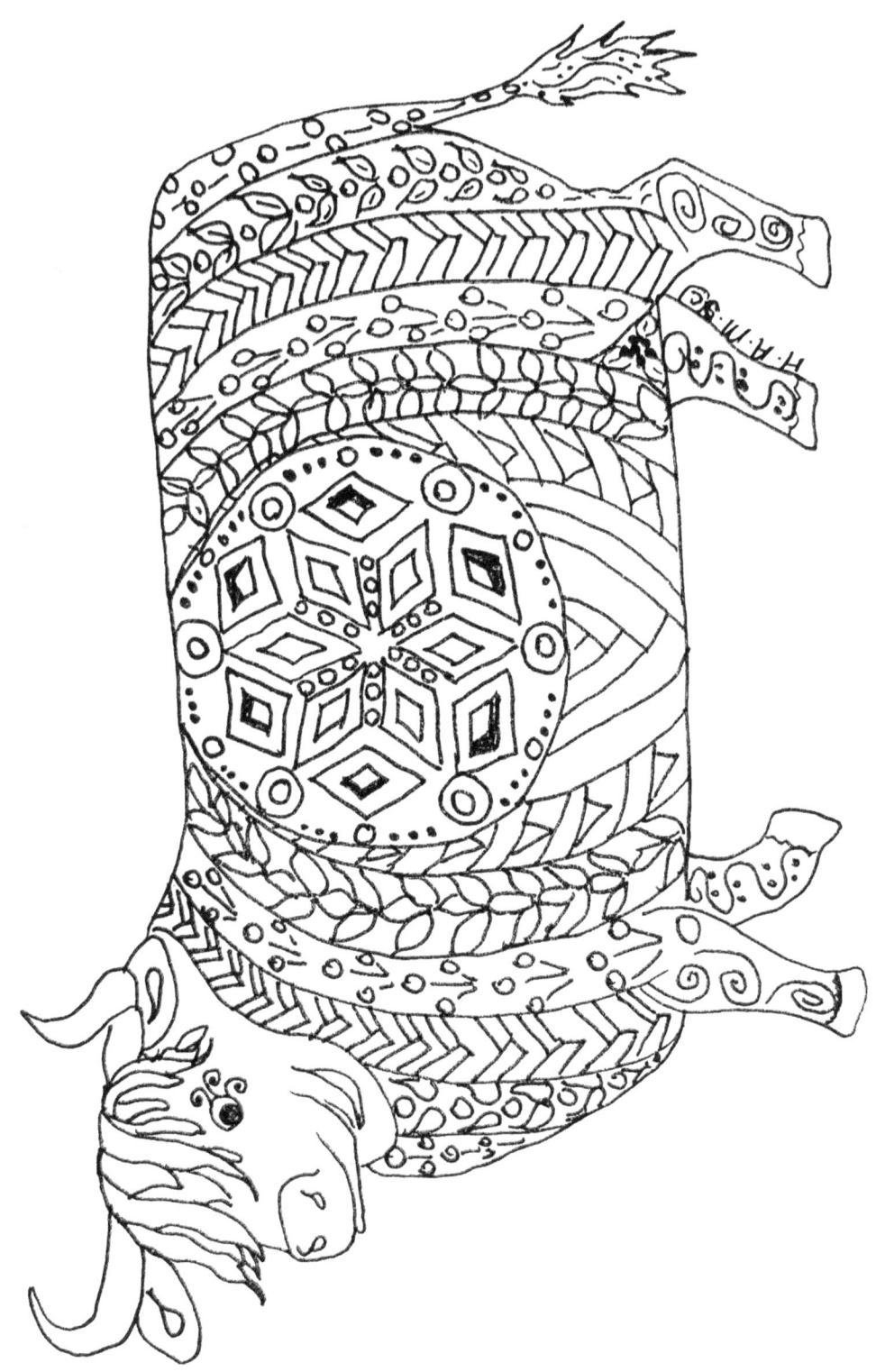

HAPPY FARM COW

BUTTERFLY FUN

WAVES OF JOY

BUTTERFLY JOY

LEAPING DEER OF JOY

BEAUTIFUL NATURE

NATURES ZEN

THE FUN IS HERE

NATURES SMILES

FLOWERS AND BUTTERFLY JOY

PRETTY NATURE

FISH STORIES ARE THE BEST

CATCH ME IF YOU CAN

SMILES OF JOY

WILD AND FREE IS FOR ME

PONY LOVE

NATURE'S BEAUTY

BEAUTIFUL OCEAN JELLYFISH

CUTE BEAR

NATURE'S PREFECTION

PLAYFUL NATURE

SILENT BEAUTY

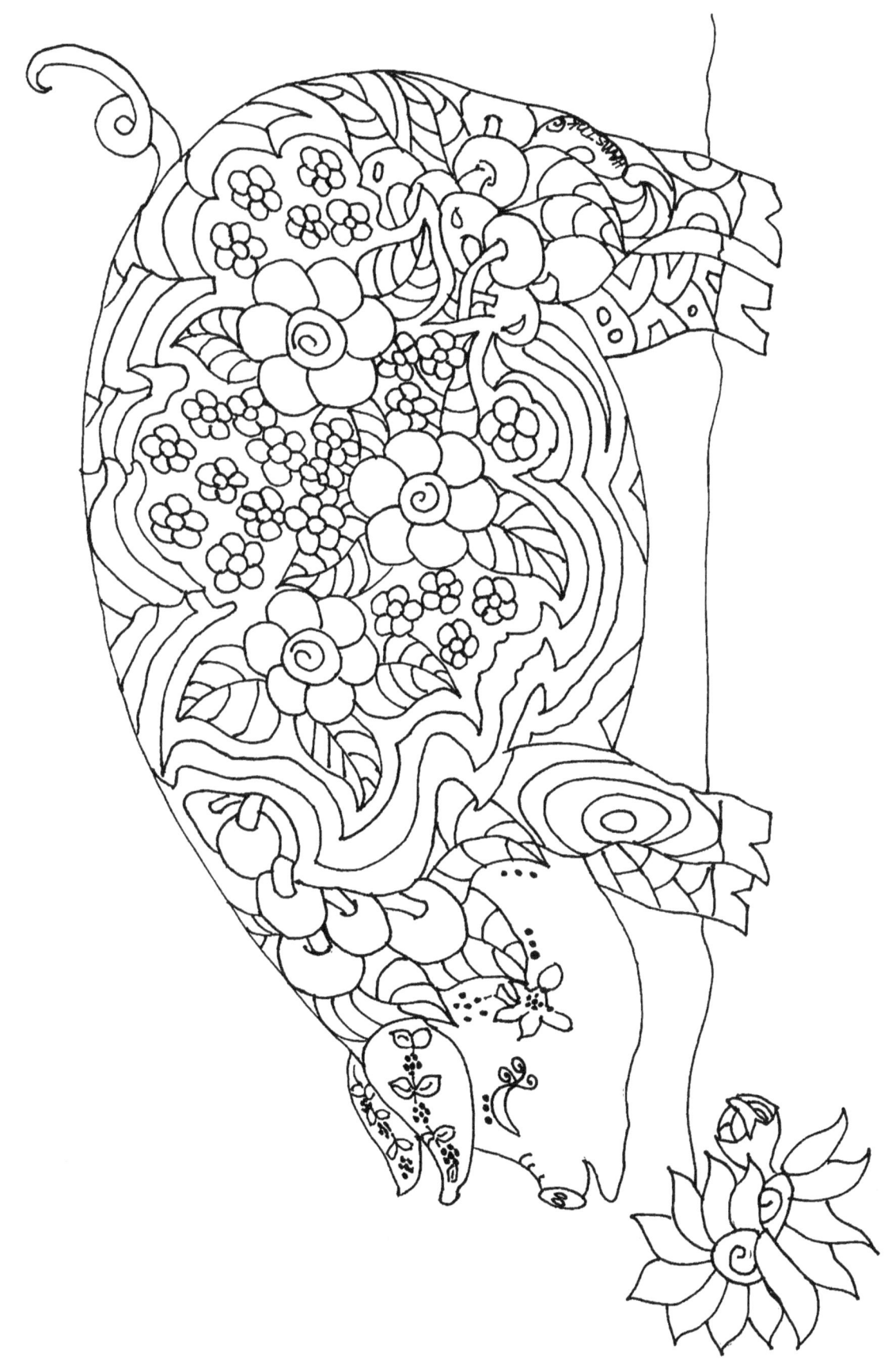

SWEET PIGGY

PUFF IT UP PUFFIN

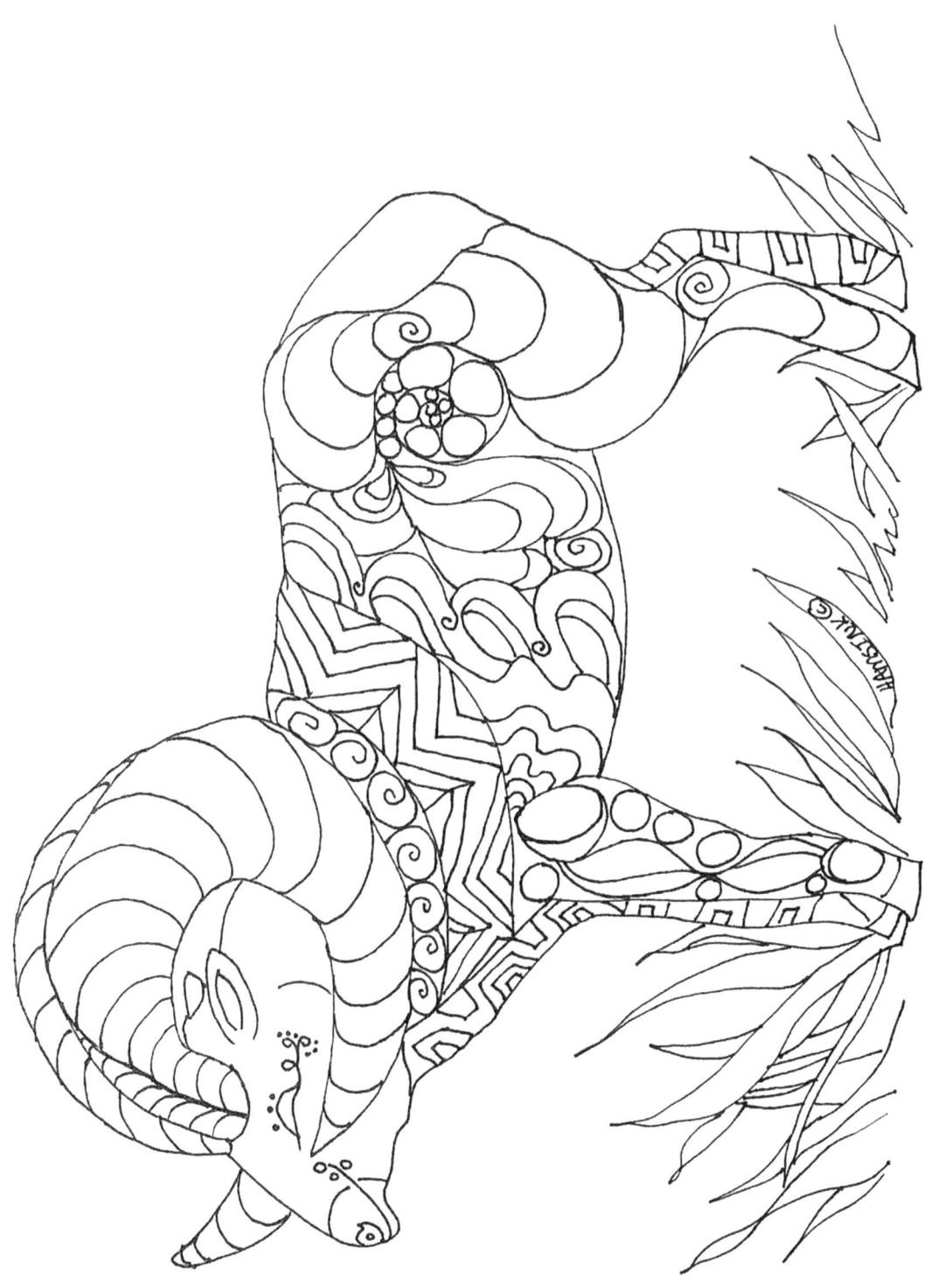

HAPPY RAM

MORINING QUAIL

SMILING SEAHORSES

FANSTATIC ROOSTER

FLUFFY BUNNY

HUNGRY SQUIRREL

SEA TURTLE

LAND TURTLE

CALL OF THE WILD

LITTLE ZEBRA

THE BANDIT OF THE FOREST

PRETTY PEACOCK

SUMMER BUTTERFLY

FLOWERS AND BUTTERFLY

SEA WHALE

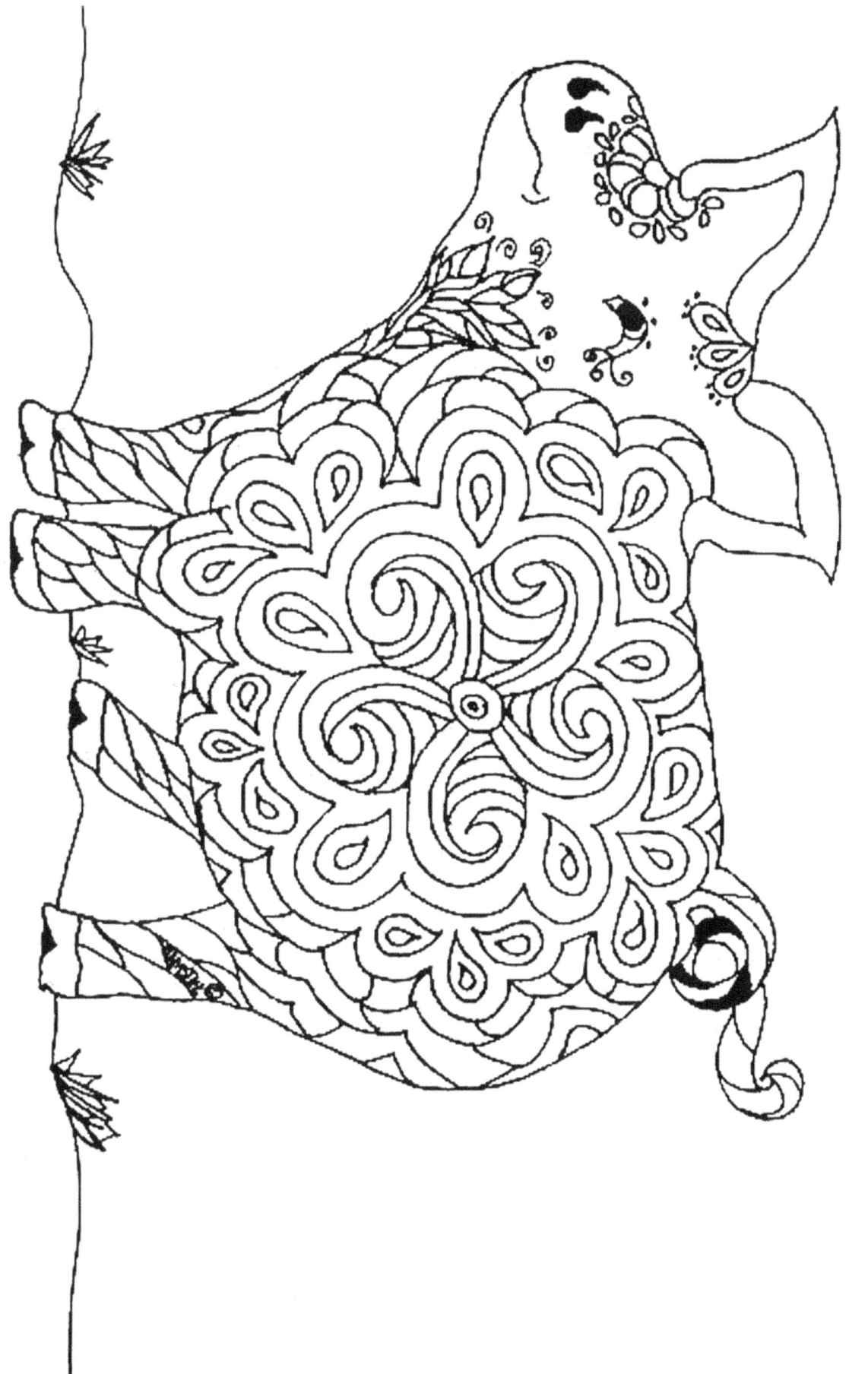

"HAPPY COLORING"

PRACTICE PAPER, TEST YOUR COL-
ORCOLORS, NOTES,

www.ingramcontent.com/pod-product-compliance
Lightning Source LLC
Chambersburg PA
CBHW080421290526
45791CB00008BA/2365

* 9 7 8 1 0 7 6 4 8 0 8 0 4 *